American Moments

ABDO
Daughters

BREAKING THE
SOUND BARRIER

By Alan Pierce

VISIT US AT
WWW.ABDOPUB.COM

Published by ABDO Publishing Company, 4940 Viking Drive, Edina, Minnesota 55435. Copyright © 2005 by Abdo Consulting Group, Inc. International copyrights reserved in all countries. No part of this book may be reproduced in any form without written permission from the publisher. ABDO & Daughters™ is a trademark and logo of ABDO Publishing Company.

Printed in the United States.

Edited by: Melanie A. Howard
Interior Production and Design: Terry Dunham Incorporated
Cover Design: Mighty Media
Photos: Corbis, Edwards Air Force Base, Library of Congress, Owls Head Transportation Museum, NASA, Smithsonian Institution, U.S. Air Force

Library of Congress Cataloging-in-Publication Data

Pierce, Alan, 1966-
    Breaking the sound barrier / Alan Pierce.
        p. cm. -- (American moments)
    Includes index.
    ISBN 1-59197-730-4
    1. Aerodynamics, Supersonic--Juvenile literature. I. Title. II. Series.

TL571.P54 2005
629.132'305--dc22

2004047696

CONTENTS

SHATTERING THE SOUND BARRIER

Before October 14, 1947, no aircraft had traveled faster than the speed of sound. Some aviation experts thought it was impossible to exceed this speed. They believed in an obstacle called the sound barrier. Experts knew that as airplanes approached the speed of sound, shock waves pounded these aircraft and in some cases destroyed them.

But not everyone thought the sound barrier was impossible to overcome. The U.S. government and military developed an aircraft specially designed to break the sound barrier. This aircraft was called the X-1. It looked like an orange bullet with wings and it was powered with a rocket engine. An army pilot named Charles "Chuck" Yeager and researchers tested the X-1 at Muroc Army Air Base in the California desert.

Chuck Yeager

THE X-1: A CLOSER LOOK

The X-1-2 research plane shown below is similar to the X-1 that broke the sound barrier. Three versions of the X-1 were built to break the sound barrier. They were the X-1-1, X-1-2, and X-1-3. The X-1-2 flew 74 missions before it was modified as the X-1E aircraft. After it was modified, the aircraft could fly twice the speed of sound.

ENGINE *four-chamber rocket engine*	
WINGSPAN *28 feet (8.5 m)*	**LENGTH** *31 feet (9.4 m)*
TOP SPEED *960 mph (1,545 km/h)*	**CREW** *1*
WEIGHT *7,000 pounds (3,175 kg)*	**YEAR MADE** *1946*

On October 14, Yeager was piloting the X-1 when it began to shake. He made adjustments to reduce the turbulence. Then the unexpected happened. The ride actually became smoother. Yet, according to an instrument in the aircraft, the X-1 had broken the sound barrier. Yeager had become the first person to fly faster than the speed of sound.

The X-1 capped the achievement by ripping the air with the first sonic boom made by an aircraft. On the ground, researchers heard the sound as it rolled across the desert. This sudden noise shattered the idea of an unyielding sound barrier.

THE SPEED OF SOUND

When Chuck Yeager broke the sound barrier, he was flying at 662 mph (1,065 km/h). The speed of sound, however, is not always this velocity. Its speed varies at different altitudes and temperatures. For example, at sea level at 59 degrees Fahrenheit (15°C), the speed of sound is about 760 mph (1,223 km/h). At 40,000 feet (12,192 m) where temperatures are colder, the speed of sound is about 660 mph (1,062 km/h).

Much of the knowledge about the speed of sound can be credited to an Austrian scientist named Ernst Mach. He was a professor of physics for many years at Charles University in Prague in the present-day Czech Republic. In 1881, Mach used photography to study projectiles such as bullets. During one experiment he photographed a bullet traveling faster than the speed of sound, or supersonic speed. This photograph

Professor Ernst Mach

A chart showing the speed of sound at different altitudes

Altitude (feet)	Altitude (meters)	Temperature (°Fahrenheit)	Temperature (°Celsius)	Speed of Sound (mph)	Speed of Sound (km/h)
0 (sea level)	0 (sea level)	59	15	761.6	1,225.6
10,000	3,048	40.6	4.8	734.9	1,182.7
15,000	4,572	5.5	-14.7	721.2	1,160.6
20,000	6,096	-12.2	-24.6	707.3	1,138.3
30,000	9,144	-47.9	-44.4	678.5	1,091.9
40,000	12,192	-76	-60	659.7	1,061.7

captured the image of the shock wave preceding the bullet. Mach was the first person to record this image.

In 1887, Mach published his study about supersonic speeds. One important idea to emerge from this work was a way to indicate speed. Mach used a number to show speed. This number is a ratio. It compares the speed of an object with the speed of sound. For example, a bullet moving at the speed of sound is traveling at Mach 1. A bullet flying at twice the speed of sound is traveling at Mach 2. The Mach number also applies to velocities below the speed of sound. An object flying at half the speed of sound is traveling at Mach 0.5.

The Mach number was later used to represent the speed of airplanes. Mach did not study airplanes, which were not invented until 1903. But the Mach number is useful for indicating supersonic flight because sound travels at different speeds.

FASTER AND FASTER

Early pilots did not need to worry about flying at the speed of sound. The first aircraft were not very fast. Two brothers from Ohio, Wilbur and Orville Wright, made the first successful airplane in 1903. But their airplane, the Wright Flyer, only had a top speed of 30 mph (48 km/h).

The development of airplanes was not limited to the United States. People in Europe began to build and fly airplanes. On July 25, 1909, French pilot Louis Blériot completed one of the most celebrated flights of the time. He became the first person to fly a heavier-than-air machine across the English Channel. During the 23.5-mile (38-km) flight, his airplane averaged 40 mph (64 km/h).

Blériot's achievement made him famous and his flight also created more excitement about airplanes. One person who recognized new opportunities in aviation was a Belgian named Armand Deperdussin. He founded Deperdussin Aviation Company, which began making faster airplanes.

One key to making faster airplanes was making a better fuselage, or main body, of an airplane.

A Wright glider in 1903

Orville Wright

Wilbur Wright

THE WRIGHT BROTHERS' HISTORIC FLIGHT

Wilbur Wright was born on April 16, 1867. His brother, Orville, was born four years later. Together, these inventive brothers created the first working airplane.

From the time they were young, Wilbur and Orville Wright were fascinated with flying. Later, the Wright brothers read about the gliding experiments of German engineer Otto Lilienthal. Lilienthal's death in 1896 motivated Wilbur and Orville to take up research into flight. By this time, the brothers operated a bicycle sale and repair business in Dayton, Ohio. Their business helped fund their aviation experiments.

After four years of testing both small models and large gliders, the brothers were ready to test powered flight. On December 17, 1903, the Wright brothers took their plane to Kill Devil Hills near Kitty Hawk, North Carolina. At 10:35 AM, Orville flew 120 feet (37 m) in 12 seconds. This brief flight made him the first person in history to fly a controllable airplane.

Fuselages of previous airplanes consisted of fabric stretched over wooden frameworks. Deperdussin's fuselages were hollow bodies of molded plywood. The new type of fuselage cut down on air resistance. This design for a fuselage is called monocoque. Fuselages today are based on this design.

The new design helped make Deperdussin airplanes among the fastest aircraft at the time. Deperdussin aircraft set speed records while winning air races in Europe. In 1913, a Deperdussin plane set a speed record of 127 mph (204 km/h).

World War I broke out in Europe in 1914. Major nations in the conflict such as Britain, France, and Germany, began to develop better airplanes to help them win the war. In 1915, the French and the Germans had discovered ways to fire machine guns through propellers. Some fighter planes had top speeds of more than 100 mph (161 km/h).

After the war, the Supermarine Company in Britain made major steps toward producing faster airplanes. In the 1920s, the company focused on making seaplanes to compete in the Schneider Trophy race. A Frenchman named Jacques Schneider organized the race to encourage improvements to seaplanes. In 1927, the Supermarine S5 aircraft won the Schneider Trophy with a speed of more than 281 mph (452 km/h). In 1931, the Supermarine's S6b won the Schneider Trophy with a speed of 340 mph (547 km/h). That same year, the S6b set a new world speed record of 407 mph (655 km/h).

The high speed reached by the S6b had an important effect on researchers who studied aviation. They realized that flying close to the speed of sound was no longer a fantasy, but a growing reality. Researchers also understood that high-speed flight presented a serious challenge. Some people began talking about a "sound barrier."

FUSELAGE DESIGN

This 1909 Blériot XI airplane demonstrates the frame-like structure of early fuselages.

The fuselage of this 1913 Deperdussin Racer displays the improved monocoque design.

The phrase "sound barrier" first appeared in 1935. It came from a discussion between reporters and British scientist W. F. Hilton. He told reporters that as an aircraft nears the speed of sound, its wings hit resistance "like a barrier." Hilton's description was reported as the sound barrier.

Sound, however, was not the problem. The real obstacle was a phenomenon called compressibility. When an airplane is in flight, it makes pressure waves that travel at the speed of sound. These waves move air out of the airplane's way. But when an airplane travels at the speed of sound, it moves at the same speed as its pressure waves. Air no longer gets out of the airplane's way. Instead, air piles up and creates shock waves. These shock waves buffet the airplane and cause the pilot to lose control. In some cases, the plane breaks up in the air.

The challenges of supersonic flight were serious enough to bring about an international meeting. In 1935, many of the best aviation engineers in the world met in Rome, Italy. Two important points emerged from this meeting. First, better wind tunnels were needed to study supersonic flight. Second, an alternative design for airplane wings might help overcome resistance near the speed of sound. German engineer Adolf Busemann was one of the first to propose a swept-back wing design to deal with air resistance at high speeds.

One motivation for studying supersonic flight at this time was the wish to build better aircraft for commercial purposes. Airplanes were being used for more than winning air races. For several years, the United States had used airplanes to transport mail. Also, in the 1930s, passenger travel by airplane had become more popular. The knowledge used to break the sound barrier could be applied to build faster, more fuel-efficient planes.

BREAKING THE SOUND BARRIER

A U.S. Navy F/A-18 Hornet jet fighter breaks the sound barrier while flying over the Pacific Ocean. Sound waves wring moisture out of the air to form the vaporous disk around the jet.

STAGE 1	STAGE 2	STAGE 3

Below the speed of sound, a plane's pressure waves move air out of the way.

At the speed of sound, air bunches up in front of an airplane.

At supersonic speeds, shock waves form a cone behind an airplane.

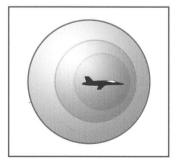
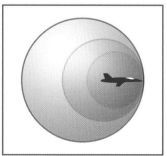
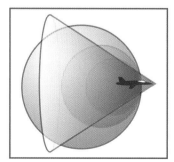

SPEEDING TOWARD WAR

In the 1930s, commercial interests were not the only factors that spurred development in aviation. Preparation for war also drove improvements in planes. Much of this development occurred in Germany, a country that had been prohibited from having an air force. After being defeated in World War I, Germany signed the Treaty of Versailles in 1919. According to the treaty, Germany was banned from building or having any military aircraft.

In 1933, Adolf Hitler and the Nazi Party came to power in Germany. As the German dictator, Hitler was determined to restore Germany's might. Part of Hitler's plan called for building up the military and creating an air force. In 1935, Hitler rejected the military restrictions of the Treaty of Versailles. That same year, Germany announced that it had an air force, called Luftwaffe in German.

As Germany built up its air force, it began to build more advanced aircraft. It also began to experience trouble with high-speed flight. In 1937, an experimental fighter plane called the Messerschmitt Bf 109 broke up in flight as the pilot attempted higher speeds.

Despite the danger of greater speeds, having faster aircraft would be an advantage. Faster bombers would be more difficult to shoot down. Fighter planes capable of greater speeds would have more success shooting down bombers.

THE MESSERSCHMITT Bf 109: A CLOSER LOOK

The Messerschmitt Bf 109 was designed in the early 1930s for a Luftwaffe fighter competition. Germany began to produce the Bf 109B series for combat in 1936. Pictured below is a Bf 109G. These planes fought the American P-51 Mustangs during World War II. After the war, Spain and Czechoslovakia continued to produce Bf 109s. To date, the Messerschmitt Bf 109 had a longer production run than any other fighter plane.

ENGINE *12-cylinder Damiler-Benz 601 Aa*			
WINGSPAN *32 feet 4 inches (9.9 m)*		**LENGTH** *28 feet 4 inches (8.6 m)*	
TOP SPEED *354 mph (570 km/h)*		**CREW** *1*	
WEIGHT *5,556 pounds (2,520 kg)*		**YEAR MADE** *1934-1958*	

The creation of a German air force alarmed Britain. Germany's new planes were better than Britain's aircraft. By the end of the 1930s, Britain introduced more modern planes into its air force.

Britain also began to experiment with a new technology called the turbojet. This engine had the potential to make faster aircraft than propeller-driven planes. Throughout the 1930s, an officer in Britain's Royal Air Force named Frank Whittle worked on an idea for a turbojet.

THE TURBOJET

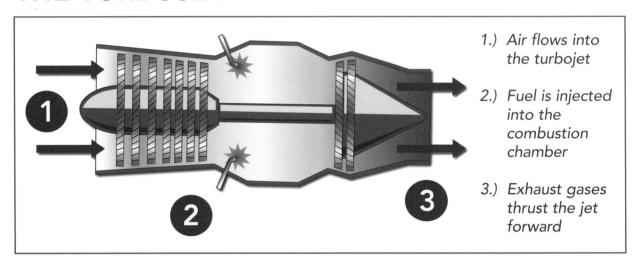

1.) Air flows into the turbojet

2.) Fuel is injected into the combustion chamber

3.) Exhaust gases thrust the jet forward

Frank Whittle (right) *explains to journalist Clifford Troke how a jet engine works.*

The British government and manufacturers did not support Whittle's idea. Companies were committed to their engine designs and did not want to change. Whittle continued his work anyway. By April 1937, he tested a prototype for a turbojet.

Meanwhile, Germany was also working on a turbojet. Aircraft designer Hans Joachim Pabst von Ohain produced a turbojet model soon after Whittle did. However, Ohain's project received more government support. Germany took the lead in jet-powered flight. On August 27, 1939, a German test pilot flew the first jet aircraft, the Heinkel He 178.

THE HEINKEL HE 178: A CLOSER LOOK

The Heinkel He 178 was the world's first jet aircraft to fly. This German airplane was an experimental aircraft only. It was not designed for long flights. The airplane was built by Ernst Heinkel, who made several kinds of planes for Germany during World War II.

ENGINE *Turbojet*			
WINGSPAN *23 feet 7 inches (7.2 m)*		**LENGTH** *24 feet 6 inches (7.5 m)*	
TOP SPEED *435 mph (700 km/h)*		**CREW** *1*	
WEIGHT *3,439 pounds (1,560 kg)*		**YEAR MADE** *1939*	

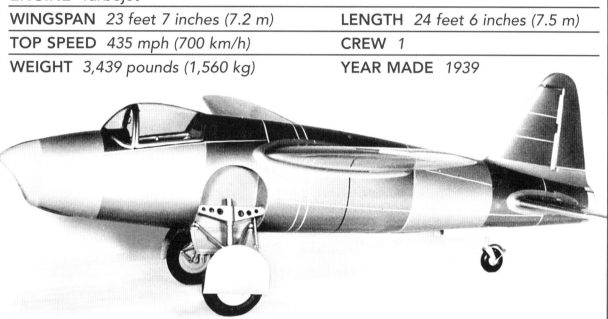

A few days after this flight, the German army invaded Poland, triggering World War II. Germany swiftly conquered Britain's ally Poland. This event was not the only troubling one for Britain. In late 1939, British spies learned about Germany's advanced secret-weapons program. Among the weapons being developed were pilotless aircraft and rockets that could deliver bombs. Britain found itself trailing behind Germany in technology.

THE DRAWING BOARD

In 1941, the United States became alerted to the realities of the sound barrier. Compressibility did not occur with jet aircraft. Instead, the trouble was with a propeller-driven airplane, the P-38. Test pilot Ralph Virden was performing a dive in a P-38 when the airplane crashed, killing Virden. Compressibility had prevented Virden from pulling out of the high-speed dive.

After the United States entered World War II, American pilots experienced more problems with compressibility. Normally, scientists could use wind tunnels to investigate aviation problems. But at this time, wind tunnels were less advanced. They provided poor information about the effects of airflow slightly below and above the speed of sound. Consequently, this tool was not useful for understanding compressibility.

Some researchers recommended the construction of a research plane to learn more about high-speed flight. Knowledge about flight near the speed of sound was becoming critical. Aviation experts knew that jet aircraft would soon fly as fast as propeller aircraft during dives. Also, the Allies had learned that Germany made significant progress with rocket-propulsion and jet-propulsion research.

Both Britain and the United States worked toward producing an experimental plane. In 1943, the British government approached

A P-38 fighter plane is loaded upon the ship USS Ranger. The P-38 was a highly successful fighter plane for the United States during World War II. However, the plane could be difficult to control in deep dives at high speeds.

WING SHAPES

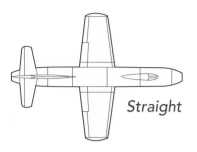

Straight

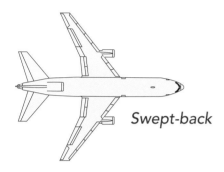

Swept-back

Variable-sweep

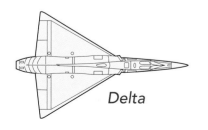

Delta

Miles Aircraft about developing a supersonic aircraft. Plans called for an experimental aircraft that could fly up to 1,000 mph (1,609 km/h) at 36,000 feet (10,973 m). Frank Whittle designed the jet engine for the airplane, called the M.52. The project encountered a setback when information captured from the Germans showed that a swept-back wing design would be more successful for high-speed flight.

Despite concerns about the wing design, the M.52 project produced some fine ideas. These ideas were similar to the ones U.S. designers used to build an experimental plane. For example, the M.52 was shaped like a bullet and had thin wings. The British project was eventually cancelled because of concerns about the safety of pilots.

In the United States, the military and the National Advisory Committee for Aeronautics (NACA) began working together to produce a research plane in March 1944. NACA and the U.S. Army Air Forces disagreed about one basic aspect of the experimental aircraft. NACA favored using a turbojet to power the airplane. The army wanted to use rocket propulsion.

The army believed that a rocket engine provided more thrust than a turbojet. An airplane with a rocket engine could reach higher altitudes. At higher altitudes, the airplane would experience less strain at higher speeds.

NACA preferred the turbojet for a few reasons. Rocket engines were dangerous because of their explosive fuels. Also, jet engines were lighter and more fuel-efficient than rocket engines.

By this time, jet engines had progressed beyond the experimental stage. In 1944, the German air force had unleashed a jet fighter, the Messerschmitt Me 262. The Messerschmitt Me 262 was slower than German test jets, but it was still capable of achieving 525 mph (845 km/h). More importantly, this German jet was about 100 mph (161 km/h) faster than Allied propeller airplanes. British pilots began flying the jet fighter Gloster Meteor in July 1944, but it was slower than the Messerschmitt Me 262.

THE ROCKET

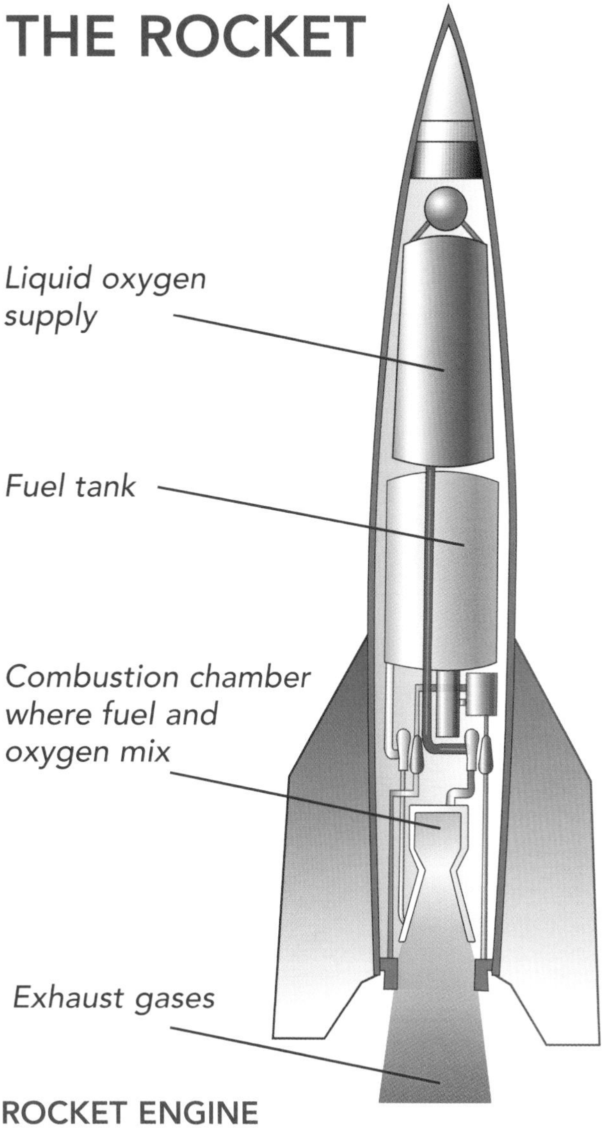

Liquid oxygen supply

Fuel tank

Combustion chamber where fuel and oxygen mix

Exhaust gases

ROCKET ENGINE
This diagram shows the basic structure of a rocket engine. A rocket engine is more powerful than a jet engine.

The bullet-shaped X-1

Despite the growing use of jet engines, the army won the argument to use a rocket engine. After all, the army was paying for the project. In March 1945, the army selected Bell Aircraft Corporation to build the research plane. Bell engineers began studying bullets because bullets were known to travel at supersonic speeds. The 0.50-caliber bullet performed especially well at this speed. Eventually, the engineers based the shape of the research plane's fuselage on the 0.50-caliber bullet.

Researchers also needed to decide whether the aircraft would have thick wings or thin ones. NACA's study supported using thin wings. Thin wings performed much better at speeds near the speed of sound. Ultimately, a design using thin wings was chosen.

Engineers decided to construct a high tail for the aircraft. This would allow the tail to move back and forth in turbulence. In addition, NACA and Bell added a stabilizer, or horizontal tail, to the aircraft. The stabilizer would be movable, which would allow the pilot more control at velocities near the sound barrier.

Bell did not design the rocket engine for the aircraft. Instead, Reaction Motors Incorporated in New Jersey made the four-chamber rocket engine. The engine produced 6,000 pounds (2,722 kg) of thrust when all four chambers were ignited. Liquid oxygen and alcohol mixed with water provided fuel for the engine. This fuel was less dangerous to handle than other rocket fuels at the time.

Another key issue was whether the experimental airplane would take off from a runway or would be launched in the air. Launching it by air meant that the research plane would be dropped from a larger aircraft, such as a bomber. If the research plane took off from a runway, fuel would be consumed during the climb to gain proper elevation. Bell decided to use the air launch so the research plane could use its fuel to achieve supersonic speed.

One problem with an air launch was that all U.S. bombers were being used in the war. But the United States and its allies were winning the war against Germany and Japan. Germany soon surrendered, and fighting in Europe ended May 8, 1945. Japan surrendered almost four months later, on September 2, 1945. Bombers were now available to launch the research plane. The U.S. Army provided a B-29 Superfortress bomber for the project.

A bomber on the ground with a smaller experimental airplane

An experimental plane being loaded into the bomber

The bomber drops an experimental plane

THE X-1

The experimental plane was originally called the XS-1 for Experimental Sonic. Later, the name was shortened to X-1. The X-1 was almost 31 feet (9.4 m) long and had a wingspan of 28 feet (8.5 m). It weighed 7,000 pounds (3,175 kg) when empty.

Bell began the X-1's test flights in January 1946. The first series of flights took place at Pinecastle Army Airfield in Orlando, Florida. These flights were not intended to break the sound barrier. In fact, the X-1 was first flown in glide flights without the rocket engine. These flights were conducted to test the air-launch method and to check the plane's responsiveness in flight.

Bell's chief test pilot, Jack Woolams, flew the X-1 in these tests. He was impressed with the airplane. Woolams said flying the X-1 gave him more enjoyment than any other aircraft.

Unfortunately, Woolams did not get to keep flying the X-1. On August 30, 1946, he died in a plane crash unrelated to the X-1 program. While preparing for an air race, his airplane plunged into Lake Ontario. The cause of the crash was never discovered.

Woolams's crash was not the only accident that affected researchers of supersonic flight. A British pilot named Geoffrey de Havilland had also attempted to break the sound barrier. He was the chief test pilot for De Havilland Aircraft Company.

Geoffrey de Havilland climbs aboard a DH.108 Swallow.

De Havilland experimented with the DH.108 Swallow airplane. This airplane featured a swept-back wing design. Swept-back wings limit drag, or resistance, that planes encounter in the air. The plane was not powerful enough to reach supersonic speed during a level flight. To break the sound barrier, it would have to dive at high speeds.

On September 27, 1946, de Havilland tested the DH.108. The plane broke up in the air and crashed into the Thames River in England. De Havilland did not survive.

Though aware of de Havilland's accident, X-1 project members decided to continue with the program. Bell selected Chalmers H. "Slick" Goodlin to replace Woolams. Goodlin was 23 years old,

25

EDWARDS AIR FORCE BASE

Many of NASA's flight projects have taken place at Dryden Research Center (left), which is located at Edwards Air Force Base. Over the years, Edwards Air Force Base has become one of the leading flight-test facilities in the world.

but he had flown for both the Royal Canadian Air Force and later the U.S. Navy during World War II.

The X-1 program did more than change pilots. Location for testing moved to Muroc Army Air Base, now called Edwards Air Force Base. The new location in southern California offered a huge benefit. It was near Rogers Dry Lake in the Mojave Desert. The lakebed is almost always dry. And its 44-square mile (114-sq km) surface provided a gigantic landing field.

Another change was the introduction of a second X-1 airplane. It was called the X-1-2, and it was essentially identical to the X-1. The X-1-2 aircraft arrived at Muroc in October 1946.

That same month, Goodlin began making glide flights in the X-1-2. A problem with cabin pressure in the X-1-2 prevented Goodlin's first glide flight. On the ground, the problem was fixed, and Goodlin completed his first successful glide in the X-1-2 on October 11. He performed two other glide flights that month.

On December 6, Goodlin attempted the first powered flight with the X-1-2. However, a valve in the fuel system froze, meaning the rocket engine could not be turned on. While the B-29 returned to land, the landing gear on the X-1-2 extended by accident. This problem threatened to cause a crash landing. Goodlin avoided a tragedy by raising the X-1-2's nose wheel during the landing.

Three days later, Goodlin flew the first powered flight of the X-1-2. The B-29 released the X-1-2 at 27,000 feet (8,230 m). Goodlin tested the rocket engine by igniting one rocket chamber and then the second chamber. He then fired all four rocket chambers. The X-1-2 bolted forward, knocking Goodlin into his seat. Goodlin shut off the rocket engine.

Then a problem arose. A light on the instrument panel indicated a fire. Goodlin radioed Richard Frost, the pilot of the chase plane, and asked if he saw a fire. Frost saw no signs of fire. Once on the ground, it was discovered that a fire had burned some wiring in the engine compartment.

On January 8, 1947, Goodlin piloted the X-1-2 on another powered flight. He flew the research plane to Mach 0.8. The aircraft shook slightly, but Goodlin reported he was in control. In the spring, Goodlin flew powered flights in the original research plane, the X-1-1.

On May 29, 1947, Goodlin flew Bell's last test flight of the X-1-2. Bell had proved that its research aircraft could be controlled at Mach 0.8. It was up to the Army Air Forces to surpass Mach 1.

CHUCK YEAGER

The Army Air Forces began looking for pilots to break the sound barrier. It soon focused on its test pilots of fighter planes. One pilot who volunteered for the X-1 program was Captain Chuck Yeager. At 24 years of age, he was a seasoned combat pilot.

Yeager grew up in Hamlin, West Virginia, where he loved to hunt in the woods. His excellent eyesight and coordination made him a successful hunter. These are also valuable traits for a fighter pilot.

In 1941, Yeager enlisted in the U.S. Army Air Corps, which was

soon renamed the U.S. Army Air Forces. By 1944, Yeager was stationed in England and flying combat missions in a P-51 Mustang. He shot down a Messerschmitt Bf 109 on March 4, 1944. The next day, Yeager was shot down over France.

The Germans, however, did not capture Yeager. Members of the French Resistance helped Yeager escape to Spain, which was not fighting in the war. He eventually returned to his air base in England, but was not allowed to fly in combat. The U.S. military was concerned about pilots who had been shot down, but escaped. These pilots

Above left: *A postcard commemorates Chuck Yeager's service in World War II.*

might reveal information about the French Resistance if they returned to combat and were captured.

Yeager, who had flown eight missions, still wanted to fly. He met with Supreme Allied Commander Dwight D. Eisenhower to present his case for returning to combat. Eisenhower later approved the request. Yeager returned to combat, downing a total of 13 enemy aircraft.

In combat, Yeager had experienced troubles with compressibility. While diving after German aircraft, Yeager's plane shook and the controls failed. The U.S. Mustang fighter planes, however, withstood shock waves better than other aircraft.

Yeager (center) *and two maintenance men stand before a P-51 Mustang fighter plane.*

Yeager's aviation skills helped him get chosen as the test pilot for the X-1-1. One of the X-1's project leaders, Colonel Albert Boyd, was impressed with Yeager. Yeager, however, was not the perfect candidate. Boyd preferred a pilot who was unmarried in case the pilot died in an accident. At the time, Yeager and his wife, Glennis, had one son named Donald. However, Yeager remained Boyd's top choice.

Yeager's marriage was no secret to those in the X-1 program. In fact, Yeager had the name *Glamorous Glennis* painted in red and white letters on the side of the X-1-1's nose. He had done something similar during the war. The shortened name *Glamorous Glen* had appeared on Yeager's fighter planes.

On August 6, 1947, Yeager performed his first glide flight in the X-1-1 at Muroc. He completed his first powered flight on August 29. During this flight, the X-1-1 reached a speed of Mach 0.85.

Glamorous Glennis *appears prominently on the X-1-1 as Yeager stands nearby.*

Yeager pilots the X-1-1.

Yeager flew faster in successive flights. But when the X-1-1 reached Mach 0.94, Yeager ran into serious trouble. The plane's controls no longer responded. He shut off the rocket engine and landed the airplane.

Once on the ground, researchers identified the problem. A shock wave had been hitting the elevator on the X-1-1's tail. The elevator controls the ability to make the plane climb or dive. Boyd and others believed the X-1-1 had reached its top speed.

Jack Ridley disagreed. He was the X-1-1's flight-test project engineer. Ridley suggested using the stabilizer to control the ability to climb or descend. Bell had designed a special stabilizer for the X-1-1 because of anticipated problems with the elevator. Ridley's ideas were tested on the ground. After satisfactory tests, Yeager flew the X-1-1 again. He found that the stabilizer allowed him to control the plane.

During another flight, a different problem occurred. Ice spread over the cockpit's windshield, blocking Yeager's view during the plane's landing. He radioed the pilot of the chase plane, Richard Frost, and explained the situation. Frost radioed instructions back and helped Yeager make a safe landing. In the future, shampoo was rubbed on the windshield to prevent ice from building up.

MACH 1.06

Yeager's troubles were not finished. While taking a break from flying, Yeager decided to ride horses with Glennis at a nearby ranch. Yeager's horse hit a gate, throwing Yeager off. He broke two ribs in the fall. A local doctor treated the ribs, but Yeager did not tell Colonel Boyd about the accident.

Despite his pain, Yeager was determined to fly the X-1-1. His biggest obstacle was shutting and locking the cockpit door. He found he could shut the door by using a piece of a broomstick to lift the door handle.

On the morning of October 14, 1947, Yeager met with NACA engineers to discuss that day's flight. The goal was Mach 0.96. A little later than 10 AM, the B-29 bomber carried the X-1-1 into the sky. At 20,000 feet (6,096 m), the bomber released the X-1-1.

Yeager quickly powered the rocket chambers two at a time. All four worked. With only two chambers ignited, the X-1-1 blasted away from the B-29 and the chase plane. Yeager fired all four rocket chambers and climbed to 35,000 feet (10,668 m).

At Mach 0.88, the X-1-1 began to buffet. Yeager used the stabilizer to maintain control. He shut off two rocket chambers and soared to 40,000 feet (12,192 m). With less than one-third of his fuel remaining, Yeager fired the third rocket chamber.

Opposite page: *Chuck Yeager holding a model of the X-1*

Chuck Yeager and the X-1-1 exceed the speed of sound for the first time in the history of flight.

The X-1-1 climbed to 42,000 feet (12,802 m). According to the needle on the Machmeter, the X-1-1 was rushing along at Mach 0.96. Then the needle swung out of range. Yeager broke the sound barrier at 662 mph (1,065 km/h). Flying even faster, the X-1-1 hit a top speed of 700 mph (1,127 km/h), or Mach 1.06, for 20 seconds.

Flying at supersonic speeds made for a surprisingly smooth ride. Yeager was a little disappointed by the calm. He thought that breaking the sound barrier would be more sensational. The ride became smooth because the shock waves affected the airplane differently at supersonic speeds. These waves formed an invisible cone that trailed behind the X-1-1. The cone is invisible, but people on the ground experience it as a sonic boom.

Sound is caused by changes in air pressure. A shock wave is a quick and large change in air pressure that travels to the ground, where it is heard as a sonic boom. This is similar to thunder. When this cone hits the ground, it changes the air pressure and causes a sonic boom.

Despite the historic importance of Yeager's achievement, few people knew about the successful flight. NACA and the military

Chuck Yeager and Arthur "Kit" Murray paint their accomplishments on the side of the X-1A. Yeager set a speed record in the X-1A, and Murray set an altitude record in the aircraft. The X-1A was similar to other X-1 airplanes. However, the X-1A was designed to research flight at speeds greater than Mach 2.

waited to announce that Yeager had broken the sound barrier. The reason for the delay was secrecy. The United States wanted to prevent other countries from learning about the tail design needed for supersonic flight.

The Soviet Union was one country that especially worried the United States. The two countries had been allies during World War II, but now had become rivals. Even during the war, the Soviet Union had spied on the United States. The Soviet Union was interested in the United States' military technology.

Still, Yeager received recognition for his accomplishment. In 1948, President Harry S. Truman presented Yeager with the Collier Trophy. The trophy is given for outstanding achievements that improve aircraft.

In June 1948, NACA and the military confirmed the news that the sound barrier had been broken. The publicity made Yeager a hero. He appeared on the cover of *Time* magazine. Yeager also became an important spokesman for the United States Air Force. By this time the Army Air Forces was no longer part of the army. The air force was its own separate branch of the military.

A little less than a year after Yeager's historic flight, another country broke the sound barrier. On September 9, 1948, Britain broke the sound barrier with a jet instead of an aircraft using a rocket engine.

Pilot John Derry achieved this milestone for his country. But he had not been trying to break the sound barrier. He flew a De Havilland DH.108 as part of a test to study swept-back wings. During a dive, the jet went out of control, but Derry recovered and the jet reached a speed between Mach 1 and Mach 1.1.

DID YOU KNOW?

Jacqueline Cochran

Did you know that Jacqueline Cochran became the first woman to break the sound barrier?

In May 1953, Cochran piloted an F-86 Sabre jet at Rogers Dry Lake to become the first woman to break the sound barrier. Chuck Yeager flew beside her during this milestone.

As a child, Cochran stopped attending school after third grade to work in cotton mills and beauty shops. In 1935, she started Jacqueline Cochran Cosmetics. By this time, she had earned her pilot's license. Cochran hoped to save money by flying herself on business trips. She soon discovered that she enjoyed flying.

Cochran entered and won the Bendix Transcontinental Air Race from Los Angeles, California, to Cleveland, Ohio, in 1938. This began her record-setting career as a pilot. The International League of Aviators gave Cochran the Harmon Trophy for most outstanding female pilot every year from 1937 until 1940.

During World War II, Cochran flew missions across the Atlantic Ocean to supply the Allies with bombers. She recruited 25 other female pilots for these missions so male pilots would be freed up for combat. Cochran also organized and chaired the Women Air Force Service Pilots (WASPs) in 1943.

She retired from the U.S. Air Force reserves in 1970. Cochran then served as a special consultant for the National Aeronautics and Space Administration (NASA). She died in 1980. At 1,429 mph (2,300 km/h), Cochran's women's world speed record is still unbeaten.

A SUPERSONIC WORLD

Once the sound barrier was broken, American researchers worked to make aircraft that would fly even faster. The next goal was to achieve hypersonic speeds, or five times the speed of sound. In 1955, the U.S. military and North American Aviation Incorporated worked together to build a manned aircraft that would travel at hypersonic speeds. The result was the X-15.

The X-15 was tested for many years before it finally reached hypersonic speed. Like the X-1, the X-15 was launched in the air from a bomber. On June 23, 1961, the X-15 reached hypersonic speed for the first time. U.S. Air Force test pilot Robert White flew the X-15 to Mach 5.3, or 3,603 mph (5,798 km/h). Air Force Major William Knight set a speed record for the X-15 on October 3, 1967. He flew the aircraft to Mach 6.72, or 4,520 mph (7,274 km/h).

Speed was not the X-15's only distinction. The X-15 had flown almost to space. On August 22, 1963, test pilot Joseph Walker flew the X-15 to an altitude of 67 miles (108 km).

Research made during the X-15 flights contributed to the progress of the U.S. space program. For example, X-15 experiments benefited the Saturn rockets used in the Apollo program. Information learned about aerodynamics was used to design the space shuttle. Also, the X-15 program developed a pressurized suit for pilots in space.

THE X-15: A CLOSER LOOK

In June 1952, the NACA Committee on Aerodynamics recommended that the military research Mach 10 flight and altitudes of 12-50 miles (19-80 km). This proposal led to the X-15, and the first X-15 was completed in October 1958. Later, the X-15 became the fastest plane in the world.

ENGINE	*Reaction Motors, Inc. XLR11 & XLR99*		
WINGSPAN	*22 feet 4 inches (6.8 m)*	**LENGTH**	*49 feet 11 inches (15.2 m)*
TOP SPEED	*4,520 mph (7,274 km/h)*	**CREW**	*1*
WEIGHT	*11,374 pounds (5,159 kg)*	**YEAR MADE**	*1958*

One of the most famous people to wear a space suit had flown in the X-15 program. Between November 1960 and July 1962, Neil Armstrong piloted seven flights in the X-15. Soon, Armstrong became an astronaut. On July 20, 1969, he became the first person to walk on the moon.

Supersonic flight, however, isn't restricted to test pilots and astronauts. Since Yeager's and Derry's flights, many people have flown at supersonic speeds. In fact, many who have experienced supersonic flight have done so on passenger jets.

The Soviet Union built the first supersonic airliner, the Tupolev TU-144. On December 31, 1968, this supersonic jet made its first

The Concorde takes off from Heathrow Airport near London, England.

flight. The TU-144, however, did not have a successful record. In the 1970s, the TU-144 crashed twice, and by the early 1980s it was no longer flying.

A more successful supersonic passenger jet was the Concorde. Companies from Britain and France worked together to produce the jet. The Concorde made its first flight on March 2, 1969, but passenger service did not begin until January 1976.

The Concorde's supersonic speed of Mach 2 slashed the time for crossing the Atlantic Ocean. For example, in 1968, a Boeing 707 passenger jet took 6 hours and 40 minutes to fly from New York, United States, to London, England. In 1974, the Concorde flew from London to New York in 2 hours and 56 minutes.

But fantastic speed did not mean incredible profits for the airlines that flew the Concorde. In fact, the Concorde lost money because of high operating costs. No more Concordes were built after 1979.

The Concorde later experienced a disaster on July 25, 2000. That day at Charles de Gaulle Airport in Paris, France, the Concorde crashed for the first time, killing 113 people. Three years later, British Airways and Air France announced they would no longer offer Concorde flights.

Although the Concorde has been grounded, many other supersonic aircraft dart through the sky today. These are military aircraft. Research of supersonic flight led to better designs for jet fighters. For example, F-86 Sabre jet fighters were equipped with a better tail design for supersonic flight. This design gave the F-86 an advantage over Soviet aircraft in the Korean War. U.S. pilots shot down 500 Soviet MiG-15 fighters, while losing 78 F-86s.

Supersonic fighter jets, space shuttles, and Concordes all owe their existence to the success of the X-1. Breaking the sound barrier heralded new achievements in flight near the Earth and in space. Some have pointed out that supersonic flight was not about vanquishing a physical barrier. Rather, breaking the sound barrier was about a refusal to accept limitations. As Yeager has said, the real barrier was not in the sky. It was a lack of knowledge. Yeager, Goodlin, Woolams, and a number of researchers demolished the barrier of the unknown.

The F-86 Sabre had a top speed of about 700 mph (1,127 km/h).

TIMELINE

1887 Ernst Mach publishes his study about supersonics. This research introduces a way to indicate supersonic speeds. This system is later called the Mach number.

1903 On December 17, the Wright brothers make the first successful flight in an airplane near Kitty Hawk, North Carolina.

1918 World War I ends with the German surrender to the United States, Great Britain, and France.

1919 On June 28, Germany signs the Treaty of Versailles. The treaty prohibits Germany from having an air force.

1920 The Treaty of Versailles goes into effect.

1931 The British Supermarine S6b sets a new world speed record of 407 mph (655 km/h).

1935 Aviation engineers meet in Rome, Italy, to discuss obstacles to supersonic flight.

The phrase "sound barrier" first appears. Reporters use the phrase after a discussion with British scientist W. F. Hilton.

1937 British Royal Air Force officer Frank Whittle tests a prototype for a turbojet. German designer Hans Joachim Pabst von Ohain builds a model of a turbojet soon after Whittle.

1939 On August 27, Germany tests its first jet aircraft, the Heinkel He 178.

1943 Britain begins to work on an airplane called the M.52 to break the sound barrier.

1944 In March, the National Advisory Committee for Aeronautics and U.S. military work together to develop a research plane to break the sound barrier. The project leads to the construction of the X-1 rocket plane.

1946 In January, test flights of the X-1 begin at Pinecastle Army Airfield in Orlando, Florida.

In September, pilot Geoffrey de Havilland dies in an airplane crash in England while attempting to break the sound barrier.

In October, Chalmers H. "Slick" Goodlin begins test flights of the X-1-2 at Muroc Army Air Base in California.

1947 On October 14, Captain Chuck Yeager becomes the first person to break the sound barrier. He reaches a top speed of 700 mph (1,127 km/h) in the X-1-1.

American Moments

FAST FACTS

NACA test pilot A. Scott Crossfield became the first pilot to fly at twice the speed of sound. On November 20, 1953, he flew a D-558-2 Skyrocket to Mach 2, or 1,292 mph (2,079 km/h). Crossfield made the historic flight at Edwards Air Force Base in California.

On December 12, 1953, Chuck Yeager set a speed record in another experimental aircraft, the X-1A. The aircraft reached a speed of 1,650 mph (2,655 km/h), or Mach 2.44. Yeager, however, almost died in the flight. The aircraft spun out of control and fell more than 50,000 feet (15,240 m). Yeager regained control and landed the X-1A on a lakebed.

The Lockheed SR-71A Blackbird is the fastest turbojet plane ever made. It can travel up to 2,250 mph (3,621 km/h), or Mach 3.4. The aircraft was developed as a U.S. spy plane in the 1960s.

The United States never made a supersonic passenger jet. In the 1960s, aviation companies in the United States worked on designing one. But concerns about costs kept these companies from building one. Also, some people worried that exhaust from supersonic jets might harm the Earth's ozone layer.

On October 13, 1997, the *ThrustSSC* became the first car to break the sound barrier. The British car accomplished this feat in the Nevada desert. Two days later, the car set the world land-speed record with a speed of 763 mph (1,228 km/h). The *ThrustSSC* was outfitted with two jet engines.

WEB SITES
WWW.ABDOPUB.COM

Would you like to learn more about Breaking the Sound Barrier?
Please visit **www.abdopub.com** to find up-to-date Web site links
about Breaking the Sound Barrier and other American moments.
These links are routinely monitored and updated to provide the
most current information available.

NACA aircraft: (clockwise from bottom left)
Bell X-1A, D-558-1 Skystreak, XF-92A Dart, Bell X-5,
D-558-2 Skyrocket, X-4 Bantam, X-3 Stiletto (center)

GLOSSARY

aerodynamics: the study of forces acting on objects, such as airplanes, as they move through the air. Aerodynamics also studies the motion of air.

Apollo program: the U.S. project to land astronauts on the moon. The National Aeronautics and Space Administration (NASA) conducted six moon landings between July 1969 and December 1972.

caliber: a unit of measurement for ammunition and for a gun's barrel.

coordination: muscles working together smoothly to perform a task.

dictator: a ruler who has complete control and usually governs in a cruel or unfair way.

French Resistance: a movement of secret groups dedicated to fighting Nazi Germany's occupation of France during World War II. Members of the Resistance spied on the Germans, destroyed enemy targets, and helped Allied airmen shot down over France.

Korean War: 1950 to 1953. A war between North and South Korea. The American government sent troops to help South Korea.

Machmeter: an instrument that displays the Mach number of an aircraft in flight.

monocoque: a design for a fuselage. Monocoque fuselages are more streamlined than earlier types of fuselages.

National Advisory Committee for Aeronautics (NACA): A group created in 1915 to advise the U.S. president about aircraft and flight. NACA became a leader in research about flight. In 1958, NACA was used to form the National Aeronautics and Space Administration (NASA).

Nazi Party: the organization that ruled Germany from 1933 to 1945. The Nazi Party was led by Adolf Hitler and controlled the most important features of German life.

prototype: the first version of an invention that tests an idea to see if it will work.

seaplane: an airplane that takes off and lands on water.

shock wave: pressure wave made by an object traveling at supersonic speed. Shock waves are faster than the speed of sound.

swept-back wings: wings that tilt back from the fuselage. The wing tips point toward the plane's tail.

technology: application of scientific knowledge to solve practical problems.

turbojet: a jet engine that burns a blend of air and fuel in a combustion chamber. The result produces a jet of gas that thrusts the aircraft forward.

velocity: speed.

wind tunnel: a structure used to study the effects of air movement on aircraft models.

World War I: 1914 to 1918, fought in Europe. The United States, Great Britain, France, Russia, and their allies were on one side. Germany, Austria-Hungary, and their allies were on the other side. The war began when Archduke Ferdinand of Austria was assassinated. The United States joined the war in 1917 because Germany began attacking ships that weren't involved in the war.

World War II: 1939 to 1945, fought in Europe, Asia, and Africa. The United States, France, Great Britain, the Soviet Union, and their allies were on one side. Germany, Italy, Japan, and their allies were on the other side. The war began when Germany invaded Poland. The United States entered the war in 1941 after Japan bombed Pearl Harbor, Hawaii.

INDEX